William Hall

Winner of the Victoria Cross

Bridglal Pachai

Four East Publications Ltd.
P.O. Box 29
Tantallon, Nova Scotia B0J 3J0

design and layout by Paul McCormick
printing and imagesetting by
McCurdy Printing (1995) Limited
Halifax, Nova Scotia, Canada

Acknowledgements

The publisher wishes to express his appreciation for the financial support of the **Nova Scotia Department of Education and Culture** and the **Canada Council**.

The publisher thanks particularly Mary Blackford of the Maritime Museum of the Atlantic, Halifax, N.S. and Andrew Trotman of the Royal Naval Museum, Portsmouth, England, for their help in procuring pictures.

The author acknowledges his gratitude to Richard Rogers, Four East Publishers, for the opportunity to contribute to this important series; to his friend and former colleague, Henry Bishop, Curator, Black Cultural Centre, for cooperation and information; to the staff and institution of the Provincial Museum and the Provincial Archives for information, assistance and photographs; to Rubin Thompson of the Physical Plant at Acadia University who put him on the trail of William Hall's baptismal certificate and to Dr. Leslie Oliver of Acadia University who obtained copies.

Canadian Cataloguing in Publication Data

Pachai, Bridglal.

William Hall

(Famous Canadians)
Includes bibliographical references.
ISBN 0-920427-35-9

1. Hall, William Edward, 1826-1904 — Juvenile literature.
2. Blacks — Nova Scotia — Biography — Juvenile literature.
I. Title.   II. Series: Famous Canadians (Tantallon, N.S.)

FC2350.B627   1995   j971.6'02'092   C95-950255-6
F1040.N3P32   1995

Preface

There is for all of us a fascination in discovering how people lived in the past. Most adults are familiar with questions, "What was it like when you were growing up?" and "What did you do when you were my age?" The series is intended to address this interest and make available to young people some of the material previously found only in books directed towards the adult market. Although the biographies have been kept brief, the bibliographies will suggest reading for those who would like to do further research.

These Famous Canadians who were pioneers and innovators in their day are our local heroes and heroines; the contribution they made to our way of life is recorded in our museums and historic homes. We hope that this series will increase awareness of our Canadian heritage, both for those who already live here and for visitors who may wish to stay awhile in order to get to know us and our history better.

Hilary Sircom
General Editor

Contents

Introducing William Hall 1829 - 1904

The name of William Hall deserves to be better known than it is. This is the story of a person whose roots can be traced to Africa, but who was born in Canada, near the small town of Hantsport in Nova Scotia's beautiful Annapolis Valley.

As a teenager, William Hall took to the sea and worked in Nova Scotian and American merchant vessels and the U.S. Navy before entering the service of the Royal Navy. At age 28, this young Nova Scotian displayed outstanding courage in the field of battle, thousands of kilometres from home. For this he was awarded the highest honour for bravery in the British Empire, the Victoria Cross. What a remarkable man and what a remarkable achievement!

Today, by whatever term people of African descent prefer to call themselves, such as black Nova Scotians, Afro-Nova Scotians, Afro-Canadians or African-Canadians, they are proud members of the Canadian family. Today, all Canadians are entitled to the same rights, privileges and respect whatever their racial origin. However, William Hall, who died in 1904, lived at a time when people of African descent were unjustly held in low esteem. Most of Africa was still under the control of European nations. Its people had suffered from centuries of exploitation by foreign rulers and traders who came from Europe, Asia and the Middle East, in search of slaves, ivory, gold and raw materials.

The story of William Hall is not complete as the story of one person. To be fully appreciated, his success must be seen in the con-

text of the history of black people in North America—of their arrival and settlement, of their many and long struggles for survival and advancement, of their failures and successes, of their loyalty and religion, of their courage and determination.

Africans Arrive In Nova Scotia

In order to know something about the background of William Hall one needs to know when and why members of the black population of Africa came to Nova Scotia. They did not come directly but from our southern neighbour, the United States of America. This takes us back to the story of the slave trade.

Today it is difficult to believe that once there was such a practice as the buying and selling of human beings. This took place in all parts of the world but what happened in Africa to Africans was the last, longest and most destructive example in the history of slavery and the slave trade. The years between 1450 and 1850 are the years when the greatest misery was inflicted by the forced removal of between 19 and 25 million human beings, men, women and children, from their homes in Africa to Asia, the Middle East, Europe, North America, South America and the Caribbean Islands.

In the southern states of the United States, cotton and tobacco plantations required labour; this was obtained in the form of slaves captured and transported from West Africa. Today there are over 30 million persons of African descent in the United States and about a quarter of a million in Canada. There were no cotton or tobacco plantations in Canada; how then was it that these people came to this country?

It was political events in the United States which led to this movement. Slaves were set free from time to time and those who came to Canada included both free persons as well as slaves.

Some slaves came with their owners, and some free Blacks came too, from the New England states in search of land and opportunities in neighbouring Nova Scotia.

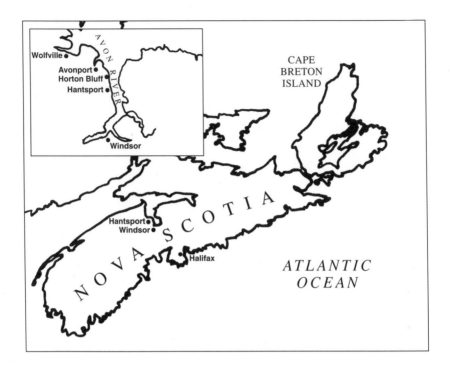

During and after the American Revolution (1776-1783) some 5,000 free and slave Blacks were brought mainly to Nova Scotia, but also in small numbers to Ontario and New Brunswick.

In 1796 about 500 Blacks called Maroons were brought from Jamaica to Nova Scotia. Some were employed in building the Halifax Citadel.

A group of about 2,000 free Blacks came to Nova Scotia as a result of the war of 1812, between the United States and Britain. It seems certain that William Hall's parents were among these people.

There were also the runaway or fugitive slaves, numbering around 40,000, who fled from the United States into Ontario helped by a secret organization known as "the underground railroad". Both black and white people, friends of the runaways, provided shelter, food and advice to slaves escaping to Canada and freedom.

William Hall: The Early Years

There are different accounts of the events that led to the arrival of William Hall's parents in Nova Scotia. One account says that they were part of the slave cargo of a ship on its way to America during the war of 1812-1814. This account says that the British seized the ship and directed it and its cargo of slaves to Halifax where the slaves were set free.

Another account states that William's father escaped from his master in Virginia during the same war and came over to the British side in return for the promise of freedom in a British territory. He would then be one of the 2,000 black refugees who came to Nova Scotia between 1812 and 1814.

What is clear, whichever account is true, is that William's parents came to Nova Scotia as a result of opportunities provided by the war of 1812. As soon as they landed in Nova Scotia they were free persons.

Documentary sources on these early years are very scarce but there is one document of considerable importance. This is the baptismal certificate of William Hall (published by the present author for the first time, in 1991, in the book entitled *Beneath The Clouds of the Promised Land: The Survival of Nova Scotia's Blacks, Volume 2, 1800-1989*). This certificate, which is located in Saint Andrew's United Church, Wolfville, provides the valuable information that William Neilson Hall was born on April 25th, 1829. As well as providing evidence of the date of his baptism, this document gives the full name of William Hall which had previously been recorded as William Edward Hall. This is how it appears on the two monuments

When Baptized.	Child's Christian Name.	Parents Name.		Abode.	Quality, Trade, or Profession.	By whom the Ceremony was performed.
		Christian.	Surname.			
1834 August 28th No. 89.	Charles Gilleon son of	Jacob & Lucinda	Hall Col. people	Horton Bluff	Mariner	W. Temple
August 28th No. 90.	William Nelson son of	Jacob & Lucinda (Col. people)	Hall	Horton Bluff	Mariner	W. Temple
August 28th No. 91.	Margaret Marina daughter of	Jacob & Lucinda	Hall Col. people	Horton Bluff	Mariner	W. Temple
August 28th No. 92.	Lucy Ann daughter of	Jacob & Lucinda	Hall Col. people	Horton Bluff	Mariner	W. Temple

Record of Baptisms in Horton, Cornwallis, August 28th 1834. William Hall is second on this page. His date of birth has been written in as April 25th 1829.

erected in his memory—one at the Hantsport Baptist Church and one at the Cornwallis Street United Baptist Church in Halifax.

As William Shakespeare wrote "What's in a name? That which we call a rose by any other name would smell as sweet." There is no debate about the heroism of this Canadian, known to the world as William Hall V.C. The rest of this book will use the name William Hall.

There had previously been some uncertainty about the date and place of William Hall's birth. Dr. Phyllis Blakeley, former Nova Sco-

Lighthouse at Horton Bluff c. 1895. It is popularly believed that William Hall's childhood home was near the site of the lighthouse.

Courtesy Public Archives of Nova Scotia.

tia provincial archivist, has suggested several possible years, and places on both sides of the Avon River. She settled for 1832, in Summerville, as this is what was given by William Hall himself in a newspaper interview in 1900. But other dates have also appeared: in April 1939, the Director of Navy Accounts of the British Admiralty in London informed the Nova Scotia Provincial Secretary of the Canadian Legion of the British Empire Service League that William Hall had given the British Admiralty his date of birth as 28 April, 1821. Another bit of information was the age on the coffin plate of the casket in which Hall was buried on 27 August, 1904. The age was stated as 78 years which would make 1826 as his year of birth. One can understand that accuracy could not be relied upon for that period of Hall's life. It is, however, popularly known that William Hall's parents had a house at Horton Bluff and that this house stood on, or

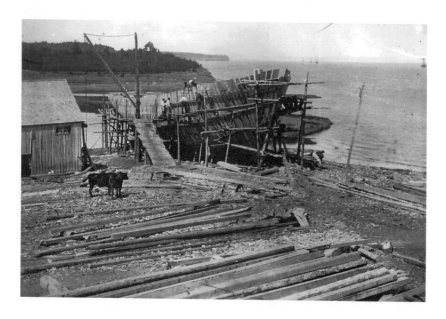

J.B. North Shipyard, Hantsport. There was employment for boys like William Hall in the local shipyards. In the picture a boat is being framed up. A yoke of oxen stands by to help move heavy timbers into place. Horton Bluff can be seen in the distance.

Courtesy Maritime Museum of the Atlantic, Halifax, Nova Scotia.

near, the site of the present Bluff Lighthouse. It was here that William Hall spent his early years and it is most likely that he was born here, one of six children.

William's parents are listed in the baptismal certificate as Jacob and Lucinda. The name Hall must have been adopted by Jacob from a white employer, as was the practice at that time. Jacob would have had many employers; among them is mentioned Sir Samuel Cunard, founder of the famous shipping line whose interests extended far beyond the shores of Nova Scotia.

At Horton Bluff one can stand on top of the ancient cliffs—well known for their interesting formations and the fossil remains to be found on the beach below—and look out to the tidal flats of the

Avon River and the Minas Basin with Blomidon in the distance. Here, between Avonport and Hantsport, was the small community where William Hall grew up. Not far away were the shipbuilding yards in Hantsport where his father worked. William no doubt spent much time there and may have had early boyhood dreams of adventure at sea.

William probably had little or no schooling. Schools were not free in those days and a combination of being poor and living a long way from the nearest school, together with the opportunity for employment in the shipyards, meant that boys such as William went to work at an early age.

In the nearby yards on the Avon River ships were built and outfitted. In 1844, at the age of 15, William Hall went to sea on one of these vessels trading with the United States. Three years later he enlisted in the United States Navy and thus launched himself on a naval career that would take him around the world. In 1848, at the age of 19, William Hall found himself in the thick of the Mexican War—the first of many in which he would serve.

While his fellow Blacks were struggling to settle and make a living in Nova Scotia, William Hall was sailing the high seas. Making a living at sea is a familiar occupation for Canadians from the Maritime provinces. However, as we have seen, in the nineteenth century life for Black people was hard and opportunities for advancement were very limited. William Hall does not seem to have been held back in his determination to get ahead. In 1852, he enlisted in the Royal Navy in Liverpool, England, and was posted to the battleship, H.M.S. *Rodney* for four years.

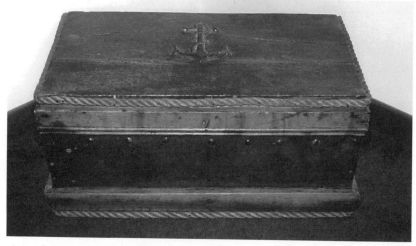

Sea-chest used by William Hall during his service in the Royal Navy.

HMS Victory. *Shown is the bow of the ship with the figurehead and the butt of the bowsprit. Although permanently in drydock, Nelson's flagship is a commissioned ship of the Royal Navy and now serves as the flagship of the Commander-in-Chief, Naval Home Command. The boy is sitting on a gun similar to those which were carried aboard* Victory *at Trafalgar.*

In The Service Of Britain

One should now pause to ask what the world was like in 1852 when William Hall became an able seaman in the Royal Navy.

The British Navy was the largest in the world. Britain was the leading industrial and trading nation with colonies and trading posts in every corner of the globe. At the height of her power, in the nineteenth century, Britain controlled a large part of the world. Her soldiers, sailors and ships were engaged in the administration of this vast empire, on land and on sea. One recalls the famous slogan of the time: "Britannia Rules the Waves". To be part of this community of strength was at the time both a challenge and an honour.

England began its overseas expansion, conquest and domination in the sixteenth century. It was the first European nation to engage in the slave trade on a large scale in that century. But it was also among the first European nations to abolish the slave trade. In 1834 all slaves in the British Empire, including Canada, were set free. But racial discrimination, based upon the strongly-held belief that European civilization was the best in the world, kept those who were not Europeans at the bottom of the ladder of opportunity. This must be understood as a fact of history. This was how it was when William Hall was in the Royal Navy. The contribution he made to the Empire and his personal accomplishments were achieved not only as a loyal British subject, born in the British colony of Nova Scotia, but as a black person handicapped by race and colour.

February 2, 1852 was a very special day in the life of William Hall, the day he turned up at the naval recruiting office in Red Cross Street in Liverpool. He was ready to begin life as a seaman in the service of Queen Victoria. Little did he know the part he would play in the making of history and that his name would be linked to that of the Queen.

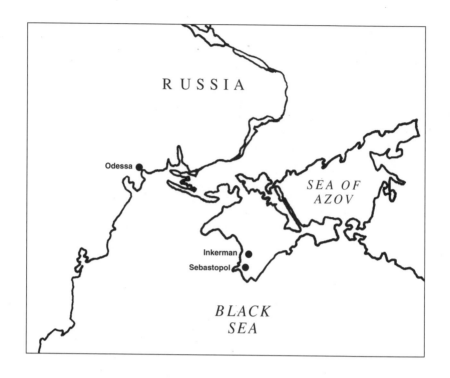

RUSSIA

Odessa

SEA OF
AZOV

Inkerman
Sebastopol

BLACK
SEA

Map of The Crimea.

In the meantime, there were ships to serve on and battles to be fought in the service of the Queen and her vast empire. William Hall was appointed to H.M.S. *Rodney* then lying at her mooring in Portsmouth harbour. The *Rodney* was one of the largest and most powerful ships in the British Navy. While this ship was waiting to return to duty in the English Channel, the new naval recruits were billeted and received training in H.M.S. *Victory* which was still in service. This was the famous flag ship of Admiral Horatio Nelson. At the Battle of Trafalgar, in 1805, Admiral Nelson's fleet defeated the combined fleets of France and Spain in one of the greatest naval battles of history. To have actually stayed aboard this ship was to have walked in the footsteps of one of the world's best known naval heroes.

For the first two years while Able Seaman William Hall served in H.M.S. *Rodney* which was guarding the English Channel from

Sailors' Encampment before Sebastopol. This is a contemporary sketch of a naval guncrew in action. The gun has been brought ashore from their ship, HMS Tiger and the crew is preparing it for firing. In the foreground are different types of ammunition. The one on the left (two smaller balls chained together) when fired spun through the air and caused great damage.

enemy invasion, trouble was brewing between Turkey and Russia who were competing for control of the Crimean peninsula and the Black Sea. The control of seaways was vital to the interests of the great powers. To achieve this control, partnerships and alliances were made among them. In the case of the Crimea, Britain and France supported Turkey against Russia; British ships, sailors and soldiers were all involved in the conflict which followed.

William Hall distinguished himself in the Crimean War. He took part in the naval brigade in which sailors joined foot soldiers to do battle on land. The sailors provided supplies, helped keep up the cannon and artillery fire, and did whatever was required of men in

William Hall's other Medals. Left to right: 1 and 2, Crimean medals presented by Queen Victoria; Hall was awarded two of these with different bars. The reverse 1 and obverse 2 are shown. 3, Medal presented by the Turkish government after the Crimean War. 4, Indian Mutiny Medal.

Photo: J. Sircom. Courtesy Black Cultural Centre for Nova Scotia.

battle. William Hall took part in two of the fiercest campaigns of the Crimean War: the bombardment of Odessa and the siege of Sebastopol. For both of these he received British campaign medals. A third medal came from the grateful government of Turkey.

In St. Paul's cemetery in Halifax there are monuments to two Nova Scotians who were with William Hall in the Crimean War. They are Captain William Parker and Major Augustus Welsford. There is no monument to William Hall here but there is one on the grounds of the Baptist Church in Hantsport, not far from where he was born and where his journey to glory began.

The Road to Glory

During the Crimean War, William Hall found out what it was like to be in the thick of battle. He saw how gallant men risked life and limb in the defense of their national honour. He saw how one of his fellow seamen, William Hewitt, defied an order to retreat and stood his ground as the enemy attacked. Hall must have been inspired by the heroism of his comrade whose action earned him the highest award for valour in the British Empire—the Victoria Cross.

The Crimean War ended in 1856 and William Hall was transferred to H.M.S. *Shannon*. This frigate was part of the British fleet on active service in the far east which was given the responsibility of protecting British interests in the area.

To understand this responsibility one has to turn back the pages of history some five hundred years. When Europeans learned of the fabulous wealth of Africa and Asia—gold, silk, spices, ivory, gems and porcelain—courageous seamen set forth on hazardous voyages of discovery. Their aim was to claim land for their monarchs and fame and fortune for themselves.

Later on, trading companies were formed and given licenses by European Kings and Queens to trade in both the east and the west. In the story of William Hall, we are concerned with the British in the east and the famous East India Company founded in 1600.

For more than a hundred years the East India Company had been ruling India in the name of Britain. The company extracted India's wealth and exported it to England. Rightly or wrongly, many of the British believed that the Indian people were better off under British rule than under that of their own princes who were frequently

Two ships in which William Hall served:. HMS Rodney (top) and HMS Shannon (bottom) off Calcutta.

A Scene in the First Voyage of the Shannon *under Captain Sir William Peel V.C. The picture, which depicts the rescue of a man overboard, commemorates the new Clifford's Boat Launching Gear. This enabled a boat to be quickly and easily launched from a vessel under full sail. The original caption states that "Hall, the black seaman standing up, won the Victoria Cross in India for bravery." The picture was dedicated to the officers and men of HMS Shannon in memory of Captain Peel who also won the V.C. He was the commander of the* Shannon *Naval Brigade in India and died there.*

Photo: J. Sircom. Taken from a print of an original picture by E. Hayes.
Courtesy Black Cultural Centre for Nova Scotia.

at war with each other. However, the British were foreigners in India and it seemed to the Indian people that in many areas company administrators, officials and soldiers governed with little regard for the welfare of the local inhabitants. There was at that time growing resentment against the British which was inflamed by the local Indian leaders.

The British, although heavily armed, were few in number and depended upon the loyalty of the Indian troops called sepoys. Dissatisfaction was growing among these soldiers. Whatever their personal grievances, they were united in a desire for freedom from their foreign overlords. All they needed were excuses to rebel. One of these came quite by chance.

A rumour was circulating that the cartridges to be used in the new Enfield rifles were greased with animal fat—the fat of pigs and cows. Two of India's great religions are Islam and Hinduism. To Muslims pig meat is forbidden and Hindus revere the cow. To touch the grease, let alone bite off the cover of the cartridges before loading the guns, would be impossible for sepoys of either faith. They laid down their arms. When ordered to obey, they refused and took up positions against the Company.

Muslims and Hindus united using religion as a bond and patriotism and nationalism as rallying cries. They were patriots fighting in the name of freedom. To the Company they were rebels and their action amounted to a mutiny.

The Company was in serious trouble. It appealed to the British Government for help. The Government asked the navy to transport soldiers, sailors and supplies to end the mutiny and restore British interests in India. The *Shannon*, stationed in Hong Kong, was one of the ships directed to sail to India and William Hall, now a Leading Gunner and promoted to the position of captain of the foretop, was among those summoned to duty.

William Hall V.C.

By April 1857, the situation in northern India was chaotic. Law and order had broken down and the rebel forces were gaining ground. By summer British ships from near and far were assembling at Calcutta. This was the largest city and the main port in northeastern India and it was here that the headquarters of the East India Company were located. However, the centre of the fighting was far inland in such towns as Cawnpore and Lucknow, over 1,200 kilometres from Calcutta.

As in the Crimean War, marines and sailors were sent from their ships to fight ashore with the soldiers. William Hall was part of the force made up from the crews of H.M.S. *Shannon* and H.M.S. *Pearl* under the command of Captain Sir William Peel, son of a former prime minister of Great Britain. For the "Peel Brigade", as it became known, it was a long and dangerous journey by river and land to get to where the reinforcements were most needed.

Leaving Calcutta in August 1857, the men and their heavy cannons were towed by barge up the Ganges River. In September they began to encounter rebel forces. By the end of October they had reached Cawnpore and from then on there were skirmishes and fighting on all sides. The Brigade passed scenes of terrible desolation where heavy fighting and the massacre of innocent civilians had taken place.

What did the young man from Hantsport think as, in mid-November, he marched with his companions towards the town of Lucknow? It was all in the line of duty . . . and Hall did his duty exceptionally well! On November 16th, 1857 he took part in the relief of Lucknow.

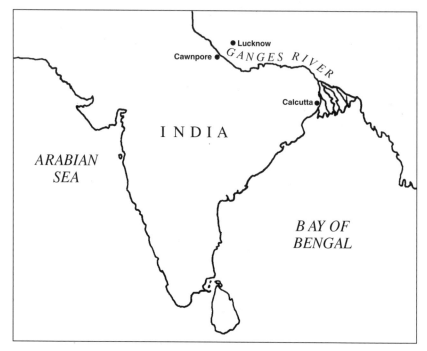

Map of India

Rebel forces were in control of the town and had laid siege to the buildings known as the Residency in which the British soldiers, together with Company officials and their families, had gathered to fight for their lives. For three months they had been under siege. During this time there had been many attempts to break down the defenses, enter the town and expel the rebels—all without success.

The *Shannon* party was made up of 250 seamen and marines, equipped with naval cannons which fired 68 and 24 pound shells. A gun crew consisted of six men. Hall was assigned to the crew of one of the 24 pounders.

About a kilometre to the west of the town of Lucknow stood a large mosque, a place of worship for Muslims, Shah Nujjif. Surrounded by thick stone walls, it was strongly fortified and the rebels were well armed, returning fire for fire. This strategic fortress prevented the British forces from gaining entry into the walled town. Its

24

The Assault on Shah Nujjif. This is a photograph of the diorama in the Royal Naval Museum, which depicts the assault on the walls of the fortress. Two naval guncrews are shown in action in the centre foreground. Before long only one gun would remain in action, manned by Hall and the wounded Lieutenant Young, who were the only survivors of these two crews.

capture was essential if Lucknow were to be relieved and the besieged garrison and civilians rescued. The infantry had made several attacks but were driven back with heavy losses each time. The walls of the mosque would have to be pierced before entry could be gained.

The *Shannon's* guns had been brought to within 350 metres of the walls and the gun crews were themselves under fire from Shah Nujjif. They were unable to make any impression on the fortifications and suffered heavy casualties. Captain Peel decided to send two guns close up under the walls of the fortress in an attempt to force a breach. One of the gun crews was a man short. William Hall who had been in charge of another gun volunteered to fill the place. Reminded that this service was beyond the call of duty and warned that it meant almost certain death, Hall still insisted on going forward with the gun.

The Relief of Lucknow. A contemporary print shows the relief of the Residency at Lucknow.

Photo: J. Sircom. Courtesy Black Cultural Centre for Nova Scotia.

The rebels concentrated their fire on the two 24 pounders. Soon the entire crew of one gun were killed and the only survivors of the other six man crew were William Hall and his officer, Lieut. James Young, who was badly wounded. Hall was a very strong man and he kept up a steady fire dragging the heavy cannon backward and forward each time he loaded and reloaded. Bullets were flying all around him, but William Hall went on sending shot after shot until at last the wall was breached, giving the soldiers enough room to scramble through.

A further nine days of fighting would be required before the sepoys were defeated and the siege lifted but the capture of this key position opened up the way into Lucknow. Sir Colin Campbell, Commander-in-Chief of the British relief force, described William Hall's gallant effort as "an action almost unexampled in war." Lieutenant Nowell Salmon, later Captain, who was also one of *Shannon's* ship's company, said of Hall that "he was a fine powerful man and as steady as a rock under fire."

Of the *Shannon* brigade on that fateful day, four heroes gained recognition for their courage. In the *London Gazette* of December 24th, 1858 the names of Lieutenant Nowell Salmon and Boatswain's Mate John Harris were listed as two members of the *Shannon* brigade who were awarded the Victoria Cross for outstanding bravery. They had climbed a tree overlooking Shah Nujjif and fired down at the rebels behind the walls.

On February 15th, 1859 the same publication announced the award of the Victoria Cross to two more heroes—Lieutenant Thomas James Young and William Hall, Able Seaman, for gallant handling of a twenty-four pounder at Lucknow, India, on November 16th, 1857.

William Hall was the third Canadian to be awarded the Victoria Cross. The two who came before him were Colonel Alexander Dunn, a native of Toronto, for valour during the Crimean War and Surgeon Herbert T. Reade, for service in Delhi in 1857, also during the Indian Mutiny. William Hall was the first Canadian seaman, the first Nova Scotian and the first person of African descent to win this highest award for bravery in the British Empire.

Some eighty Canadians have won the Victoria Cross since it was instituted by Queen Victoria in 1856. Thus William Hall is in distinguished company. While one does not make comparisons between heroes—because heroes are heroes—the point can be made that for William Hall the road to fame was not an easy one, neither would be the road to come.

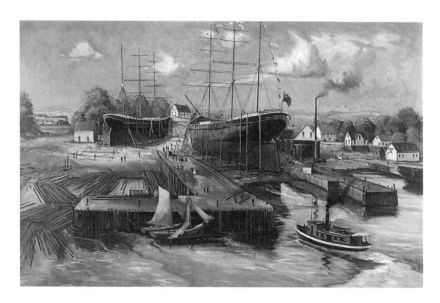

Churchill Shipyards, Hantsport, in 1873. William Hall returned to nearby Avonport in 1876. Activity on the waterfront such as a ship launching must have been of great interest to the old seamen.

Courtesy J. J. Jodrey. Photo: B. McCall

Retirement of a Hero

It was a wonderful day for the man from Hantsport when, on October 28th, 1859, he was presented with the Victoria Cross on board H.M.S. *Donegal* in Queenstown, Ireland, by Rear Admiral Charles Talbot. William Hall was just thirty years old, still a young man but mature beyond his years in travel, adventure and achievements. It is interesting to speculate how far he might have gone in his naval career if he had had more book learning. However, because of his fine service, he rose as far as a non-commissioned officer could go. He retired at the end of his career in the Royal Navy, in 1876, with the rank of First Class Petty Officer.

This was no small achievement given his humble background and the racial prejudice of the time. It must stand as a matter of considerable pride that William Hall saw active service in the Royal Navy for almost twenty-three years. He was discharged with a good conduct certificate.

Dr. Phyllis Blakeley, one of the few authors who has written about the life of William Hall, tells us that on his retirement from the navy some tradition suggests that he was offered a well paid position in Whitehall. Hall, so the account goes, declined this offer. There was another call more pressing, the call to come home, to join his sisters, to walk the pastures of the Annapolis Valley and recall childhood memories. At 47 he still had years of active life ahead of him. It was time to come home.

When William Hall returned to Nova Scotia he settled on his own farm on the Bluff Road at Avonport, Kings County. It was more than 30 years since he had gone away to sea. There are no records to

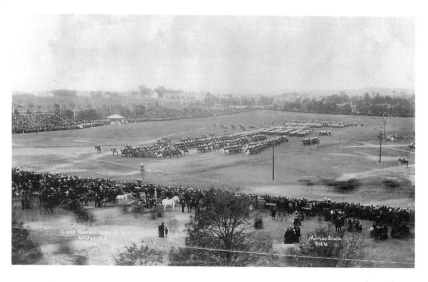

Grand Review by the Duke of York on the Halifax Commons (October 1901). William Hall was among the distinguished veterans on parade and was presented to the Duke.

Courtesy Public Archives of Nova Scotia

show that he returned home for a visit in all those years. It seems very unlikely, given the nature of his duties in distant parts of the world.

He did, however, come close in 1860 when he was a crew member of the warship H.M.S. *Hero* which brought the Prince of Wales, later King Edward VII to Halifax. He was the only one among all the veteran crew to have been awarded the Victoria Cross. Dr. Blakeley has recorded that one of the white crew members recalled part of that occasion in the following words: "We had one Victoria Cross man amongst them; curious to say, he was a Negro, by name William Hall. V.C.'s were not so plentiful then as they are now."

It was an irony of the life and times of William Hall V.C. that to many he was "a curiosity and a Negro." Only to a very few was he truly a hero. But on his native soil in Avonport, only a few kilometres

The Farmhouse in Avonport where William Hall lived with his sisters

Courtesy Public Archives of Nova Scotia

from where he had been born, William Hall was lord and master. Although he had few worldly possessions he had his pride and his dignity.

His farm was small but, according to a reporter who interviewed William Hall in 1900, it was well stocked with cattle and poultry. An orchard of about one hectare in size was well laid out adjoining his modest house. In these surrounding William Hall lived with his sisters, Rachel Robinson and Mary Hall, "away from the madding crowds ignoble strife", as the English poet, Thomas Gray, would put it.

William Hall supported himself and his two sisters on a modest pension. He led a quiet life and except for friends and acquaintances in the area received few visitors. The hero who had brought glory to Nova Scotia and Canada seemed to have been forgotten. There was

The Hero Proudly Displays his Medals.

A Rare Picture of William Hall—shown as the driver of the carriage.

William Hall's funeral procession.

however one brief moment of recognition for this man, three years before he died.

In October 1901, the Duke and Duchess of Cornwall and York, later to become King George V and Queen Mary, visited Halifax as guests of the Royal British Veterans. William Hall was one of the most distinguished among the veterans. He stood among his peers on parade with his medals proudly displayed: the Crimean Medal with clasps for Inkerman and Sebastopol; the Turkish Medal for service in the Crimea; the Indian Mutiny Medal with bars for Lucknow and the Relief of Lucknow, and, shining, conspicuously amongst them all, the distinguished Victoria Cross. The royal guests paused as they reached William Hall. The future King and Queen shook his hand, acknowledging with this public display of appreciation that he had served the Empire well. Then the Duke arranged for Hall to ride in a carriage in the procession and to be given a place of honour in the following ceremonies.

Alas, neither his province nor his country accorded William Hall any such display of appreciation during his retirement years. He died in obscurity at his home in Avonport on August 25th, 1904 at the age of 75. Two days later he was buried without honours, military or civilian, in the Baptist Church Cemetery at Stoney Hill, Lockhartville. Friends and neighbours formed a modest funeral procession to pay their last respects to their hometown hero. It was the Reverend B.D. Knott, preaching a month later in the Baptist Church in Brooklyn, where William Hall had often worshipped, who paid him the following tribute: "He was a peaceable God-fearing citizen. He was honoured and respected by all who knew him. He was ever humble,"

From Past To Present

William Hall V.C. left a rich historical legend but he died a poor man. His farm was in debt to the tune of some five hundred pounds sterling which was a tremendous sum for that time. In the hope that they could be sold to raise money to settle his debts, William Hall's medals were entrusted to a family friend, Dr. Henry Chipman of Grand Pré.

The Governor General of Canada advised Dr. Chipman that the Nova Scotia Historical Society might be interested in the worthwhile purchase, failing which the matter should be referred to the Guards' Club in London. This is what happened and thus it was that a part of Nova Scotia's historical inheritance was transferred to London.

During Canada's centenary year, 1967, William Hall's medals were returned to this country and were given a place of honour in the Atlantic Provinces' Pavilion at Expo in Montreal. Subsequently, the Victoria Cross was acquired by the Province of Nova Scotia and placed permanently in the Provincial Museum on Summer Street in Halifax.

In 1945, the remains of William Hall were reinterred on the grounds of the Hantsport Baptist Church. This plot of land was deeded to the Canadian Legion while the town of Hantsport undertook to care for the site forever. Within two years, a memorial was erected on the burial site. This was done through the combined efforts of the Hants County Branch of the Canadian Legion, the William Hall V.C. Branch of the Canadian Legion and twenty-four

Three Churches: Stoney Hill United Baptist Church in Lockhartville (top left) in whose cemetery William Hall was first buried; West Brooklyn United Baptist Church (top right) where Rev. Knott paid tribute to the hero; and the final resting place of William Hall (bottom left) on the grounds of the Hantsport United Baptist Church.

Photos: J. Sircom

Relatives of William Hall in front of the Memorial Cairn. November 9, 1947. L-R: John Neil, Mrs. Neil, Mrs. Ethel Gibson, Thomas Gray, Mrs. Violet Ford, Edith Gray, Mrs. Lena Jefferson, James Gray.

Photo: Edith Gray

other branches. The memorial was unveiled on November 9th, 1947 by Rear-Admiral C.R.H. Taylor who said,

> "It is my proud privilege to take part in this ceremony to Canada's first naval V.C. In honour of the memory of this brave coloured seaman, whose devotion to duty in the finest tradition of the navy and the British race resulted in the saving of many British lives, I hereby unveil this memorial."

Phyllis Blakeley
Dalhousie Review, Vol. 37

These words which so clearly indicate a biased point of view can be used as a basis for the ongoing debate about prejudice and racial attitudes.

Besides the relatives of William Hall who attended the unveiling ceremony, and whose picture appears in this book, one notable black Nova Scotian was on the official programme to give the benediction. He was the Reverend W.P. Oliver, listed on the programme as Padre of the William Hall V.C. Branch # 57. The Branch had earlier written to the organizers requesting that Reverend W.P. Oliver be given an official role in the ceremony. He was the only black Nova Scotian on the programme to pay tribute to the memory and the glory of a fellow black Nova Scotian. These two personalities, William Hall, V.C. and William Pearly Oliver personified, in different ways the greatness of the black contribution to Nova Scotia and Canada.

William Hall V.C. was first and foremost a member of the human race, an ordinary person with a humble background, who courageously met the many challenges of his fascinating life. That he was of African descent was his personal and family matter. That he was viewed by some as "a curiosity and a Negro" first and a person afterwards must surely be a lesson that attitudes must change.

Fortunately this is happening. The story of William Hall V.C. is becoming better known thanks largely to the outstanding work of the Black Cultural Centre for Nova Scotia in Westphal, Halifax County, the devotion and work of the William Hall V.C. Branch 57 of the Canadian Legion, and the Nova Scotia Provincial Museum.

The inspiration provided by the historical legacy of this outstanding man lives on in programmes associated with his name: the DaCosta-Hall Educational Programme for black students in Montreal; the William Hall, V.C. Gymnasium in Cornwallis, Nova Scotia, and the William Hall Nova Scotia Tattoo Gun Run.

A descendant of the black refugee family with roots in Africa, William Neilson Hall, as his baptismal certificate reads, has brought distinction to the whole human race.

Bibliography

Black Cultural Centre for Nova Scotia, Westphal, Nova Scotia.

Photo: J. Sircom

Blakeley, Phyllis, "William Hall, Canada's First Naval V.C.", *Dalhousie Review*, Volume 37, Autumn, 1957.

Clowes, W.L., *The Royal Navy*, Sampson, Law, Marstan and Company, London, 1903.

Creagh, O'Moore, *The V.C. and D.S.O.*, Standard Art Book Company, Paternoster Row, London.

Fergusson, Charles Bruce, "William Hall, V.C.", *Journal of Education*, Nova Scotia, December, 1957.

Pachai, Bridglal, *Beneath the Clouds of the Promised Land: The Survival of Nova Scotia's Blacks, Vol, II, 1800-1989*, Black Educators Association, Halifax, 1991.

Pachai, Bridglal, *William Hall, Dictionary of Canadian Biography*, Volume XIII, 1901 to 1910, University of Toronto Press, 1994, pp. 433-434.

Warner, P.V., "A Canadian Negro V.C.", *Canadian Magazine*, Vol. XIII, No. 2, June 1901, pp. 113-116.